Heal Your Heart in Thirty Days

Thirty days of guided prompts for self love, clarity and relationship recovery author: Eden Clarke

Eden Clarke

Heal Your Heart
In Thirty Days

*Thirty days of guided prompts for self love,
clarity and relationship recovery*

Eden Clarke

Contents

Welcome!   vii
How to Use This Journal   ix
The Science of Emotional Reset   xi

Part 1
Prepare for Your Journey

Your Starting Point   3
Your Intentions for the Next Thirty Days   7

Part 2
The Thirty Day Heart Reset

WEEK ONE. Awareness and Truth   13
WEEK TWO. Healing and Release   23
WEEK THREE. Rebuilding Self Worth   31
WEEK FOUR. Choosing Healthier Love   41

Part 3
Completion and Integration

Your Thirty Day Reflection   55
Your New Self Worth Blueprint   63
Your Next Steps   69

About the Author   75
Notes Pages   77

Welcome!

There are moments in life when the heart grows tired from holding too much. Old disappointments linger in the background, familiar patterns keep repeating and a quiet ache settles in where confidence once lived. A heart reset is the choice to pause, breathe and begin again with honesty and compassion. It is not about fixing yourself or rushing to feel better. It is about loosening the weight around your emotions so you can see yourself clearly and treat your inner world with more kindness.

> Emotional healing begins the moment you decide to listen to your own needs.

Sometimes it looks like releasing the beliefs that have kept you small. Sometimes it looks like admitting what has hurt you so you no longer carry it alone. Other times it is the gentle process of rebuilding trust with yourself, one small promise at a time. Healing is not loud or dramatic. It is steady, deliberate

Welcome!

and rooted in the belief that you deserve relationships that honor your worth.

This journal is your companion through a thirty day journey designed to bring you back to yourself. Each page offers a gentle prompt along with space to explore what rises to the surface. There is no right or wrong way to move through these reflections. You are not here to earn a grade or impress anyone. You are here to reconnect with the part of you that knows what you need and deserves to feel loved.

> Take your time.
> Let yourself write without pressure.
> Let the process feel simple and honest.

Some days you may fill the page with clarity. Other days you may offer only a few sentences. Both count. What matters is the act of showing up for yourself with curiosity and softness.

By the end of these thirty days, it is my hope that you feel lighter, clearer and more grounded in your own worth. Your heart already knows the way forward. This journal simply gives it room to speak.

How to Use This Journal

This journal is designed to fit gently into your life. Ten to fifteen minutes a day is enough to create real momentum. You can sit with it in the morning before the world asks anything of you or in the evening when you are finally able to exhale. What matters is that you choose a time that feels steady and supportive, even on the days when your heart feels a little heavy.

Each daily entry follows a simple structure. You will find a short reflection to open the door to that day's theme, followed by a guided prompt that invites you inward. There is space afterward for your thoughts, feelings, memories or realizations. Some entries end with a grounding line or affirmation to help you carry the insight with you. This design is intentional. It gives you enough guidance to feel held without limiting your voice or your process.

You are not being asked to solve everything in thirty days. You are simply creating room for emotional healing, clarity and healthier patterns in love. By noticing your thoughts, naming your needs and exploring your history with honesty, you begin to shift how you relate to yourself and others. Small reflections done consistently have a powerful way of changing the way your heart moves through the world.

Let the pages meet you exactly where you are. Show up imperfectly and without expectation. The transformation happens quietly as you return to yourself again and again. This is the beginning of a kinder and more grounded relationship with your own heart.

The Science of Emotional Reset

Emotional patterns do not form overnight. They grow out of experiences, learned responses and the stories we tell ourselves about love and belonging. Reflection is one of the most effective ways to interrupt these patterns because it brings the unconscious into the light. When you pause long enough to notice what you feel and why you react the way you do, you create space between the trigger and the response. That space is where change becomes possible. It allows you to choose differently instead of repeating a familiar cycle simply because it feels known.

Self worth plays a powerful role in every relationship you enter. When you believe in your value, you naturally gravitate toward connections that feel respectful and balanced. You express your needs more clearly and you step away sooner when something feels misaligned. When self worth is shaky, it becomes easier to settle for less, ignore red flags or accept dynamics that drain you. Strengthening your sense of worth shifts the entire foundation of how you give and receive love.

It becomes the quiet compass that guides you toward relationships that support your wellbeing.

Guided prompts are a helpful tool in this process because they give your mind a direction to follow. After a heartbreak or during moments of emotional confusion, it can feel difficult to know where to begin. Prompts remove that uncertainty by offering a gentle starting point. They ask questions that uncover deeper truths and help you put language around feelings you may not have fully understood. With repeated use, guided reflection helps you see your patterns clearly. That clarity is what prevents you from repeating painful dynamics and helps you build healthier ones.

An emotional reset is both a psychological process and an act of self care. It is the decision to understand yourself more deeply so your heart can move forward with strength, honesty and hope.

Part 1
Prepare for Your Journey

Your Starting Point

Before you begin the thirty day journey, take a moment to understand where you are right now. Every heart arrives at this journal carrying its own history, hopes and unanswered questions. You may feel tender, overwhelmed, hopeful or determined. You may be standing at a crossroads, recovering from heartbreak or simply longing for a deeper connection with yourself. Whatever brought you here is valid, and it deserves space to be acknowledged.

Start by noticing what has been resting quietly in your heart. There may be emotions you have pushed aside or truths you have avoided because they felt too heavy to face. Let this be the place where you finally name them. Writing them down does not make them stronger. It frees you from holding them alone.

Spend a few breaths considering what you are longing for. It might be peace after chaos, clarity after confusion or love that feels honest and safe. Allow yourself to be honest about your desires without judging them. Your longings reveal the direction your heart wants to move.

Then gently ask yourself what you are ready to release. There may be old beliefs that no longer reflect who you are becoming, memories that still ache or habits that have kept you small. You are not expected to let go all at once. Simply naming what no longer serves you begins the process.

Use this space to lay everything out with curiosity and compassion. This is the ground you will grow from over the next thirty days.

Notes

Your Intentions for the Next Thirty Days

Before you step into the rhythm of daily reflection, take time to imagine the version of yourself you are becoming. Intentions give your journey a sense of direction. They are not rules or rigid goals. They are quiet promises to your own heart, guiding you toward the growth you desire.

Begin by picturing what emotional strength would feel like for you. It might look like trusting your intuition again or staying grounded when old fears surface. It might mean speaking your truth without shrinking or choosing relationships that bring calm instead of confusion. Emotional strength is personal and it grows from within, not from pretending everything is fine. Let yourself describe what it would look like in your life.

Next, reflect on what healthier love means to you. Think beyond romance and consider every form of connection. Healthier love might feel steady, respectful and warm. It might involve clearer boundaries, honest communication or the freedom to be fully yourself. It may even mean learning to walk away from anything that consistently dims your light. Let these thoughts rise without judgement. They will become part of the foundation you build.

Finally, consider how you want to treat yourself differently over the next thirty days. Perhaps you want to speak to yourself with more kindness, slow down when you feel overwhelmed or trust your own needs instead of pushing them aside. Small shifts in how you care for yourself often create the biggest transformations. Write from a place of honesty rather than pressure.

Your intentions do not need to be perfect or complete. They simply need to reflect your truth. Let this be the moment you choose yourself with clarity and tenderness. The work you do in the coming days will grow from the intentions you set here.

Notes

Part 2
The Thirty Day Heart Reset

This section is the heart of your journey. For the next thirty days, you will gently explore the layers of your emotions, habits and hopes. Each day offers a small invitation inward so the process never feels overwhelming. You will move through reflection, clarity, release and rebuilding at a pace that respects your emotional rhythm.

Every day follows a simple pattern. It begins with a short reflection that introduces the theme and helps you settle into the right mindset. This is followed by one deep prompt that guides your writing toward a meaningful insight. After that, you will find a practical exercise designed to bring the day's lesson into your real life in a simple and achievable way. Each entry closes with an affirmation or grounding line to help you carry a feeling of strength or calm into the rest of your day.

This structure keeps the journey varied and engaging. Some days will feel light and energizing. Others may invite you to sit with feelings you have avoided. Both experiences help you grow. By returning to the page each day, you train your heart to speak honestly and your mind to listen with compassion.

Let yourself move through this section without rushing. The transformation comes through steady attention rather than intensity. These pages are here to support your healing, your clarity and the way you choose love from this point forward.

WEEK ONE.
Awareness and Truth

Awareness is the first and most essential step in emotional healing. Before you can rebuild confidence or choose healthier love, you need to understand the patterns that have shaped you. This week invites you to slow down and look inward with curiosity. You are not here to blame yourself or to analyze every detail of your past. You are here to become familiar with the truth of your own heart.

Many people move through relationships without ever pausing to ask why certain things hurt more than others or why they keep ending up in the same emotional place. Patterns form quietly. They grow out of childhood experiences, past heartbreaks, old beliefs and the ways we learned to protect ourselves. Sometimes the protection becomes the problem. Walls get too high. Boundaries disappear. Needs stay hidden. Expectations shrink.

This week gently brings those hidden parts to the surface.

You will start by noticing how your body and emotions react to specific situations. Emotional triggers are not flaws. They are signals. They show you where your heart is still tender. When you understand your triggers, you no longer feel confused by your own reactions. You begin to see the connection between past events and present feelings. This is where compassion can grow.

From there, you will explore the patterns that shaped your previous relationships. This does not mean revisiting every painful moment. Instead, you will reflect on the roles you played, the choices you made and the lessons you carried forward. Once you see your patterns clearly, you can choose differently. You can walk away sooner. You can stay aligned with your needs instead of abandoning them for the sake of connection.

Week One also guides you into understanding your limits. Many people struggle with boundaries because they were taught to prioritize the needs of others before their own. You might have said yes when you wanted to say no. You might have tolerated behavior that hurt you because you hoped things would change. You might have believed love required self sacrifice. Boundaries are not walls. They are expressions of self respect. They show the world how you expect to be treated.

Next, you will explore the needs that were never met. These needs do not make you needy. They make you human. Every person requires warmth, safety, affection, validation, presence and emotional consistency. When these needs go unmet for long periods, the heart begins to feel empty. This week creates a safe space for you to name these needs without shame. Doing so is a form of reclaiming yourself.

Another key part of awareness is listening to the voice inside your mind. The way you speak to yourself affects every area of your life. If your inner voice has been harsh or critical, you may feel unworthy of healthy love. If that voice has been shaped by past judgments or painful experiences, you may find it hard to trust or open up. By examining your self talk, you begin the work of shifting old narratives into supportive ones.

You will also reflect on what you once believed you deserved in love. Some of these beliefs may have been inherited. Others may have formed through heartbreak. You might have thought you were too much or not enough. You might have felt grateful for any attention at all. You might have accepted patterns that broke your spirit because you believed it was the best you could hope for. Acknowledging these old beliefs is an act of liberation. It allows you to rewrite your story.

The week closes by asking you to identify what is no longer serving you. This can be a habit, a belief, a fear or a way of relating to others. When you name it, you gain power over it. When you release it, even slowly, you create room for something new to grow.

Awareness can feel uncomfortable at times, but it is also deeply empowering. You are learning to understand your heart rather than judge it. You are learning to see yourself clearly. You are learning to choose truth over fear. Everything in the next chapters will build on the foundation you create this week. Allow yourself to move through these days with openness and patience. The more honest you are, the more healing will unfold.

DAY ONE. NOTICING EMOTIONAL TRIGGERS

Reflection

Every emotion carries a message. Triggers often appear in small moments, such as a tone of voice, a delay in a reply or a familiar phrase. They can also appear in larger situations that remind you of past pain. Instead of avoiding these moments, today you will pay attention to what rises inside you. Awareness allows you to understand yourself rather than react automatically.

Prompt

Write about a recent moment that stirred a strong emotion in you. Describe what you felt, when it began and what memory or belief it connected to. Let your thoughts unfold honestly.

Exercise

When you feel a strong emotion today, pause for a few breaths. Place a hand on your chest or your stomach and simply notice the sensation. Ask yourself what your emotion is trying to tell you. Do not pressure yourself to fix anything. Just listen.

Grounding line

My feelings are guides, not threats.

DAY TWO. UNDERSTANDING PAST RELATIONSHIP PATTERNS

Reflection

Patterns are repeated not because they are healthy but because they are familiar. Today you will explore recurring themes in your past relationships. This is not to blame yourself. It is to understand the emotional landscape you have been navigating.

Prompt

Think about the relationships that have shaped you. What patterns do you notice in the way you loved, the way you communicated or the way you protected yourself. Describe any similarities across different relationships.

Exercise

Choose one pattern you identified and reflect on where it might have started. Consider whether it once helped you feel safe, even if it no longer serves you now.

Grounding line

Awareness opens the door to change.

DAY THREE. IDENTIFYING LIMITS AND BOUNDARIES

Reflection

Boundaries are not about keeping people away. They are about keeping yourself protected and respected. When you lack clear boundaries, feelings of resentment and exhaustion grow. Today you will explore where your limits have been crossed and where you want to draw new lines.

Prompt

Write about a time you ignored your own limits. What did you feel during that moment. What would a healthier boundary have looked like.

Exercise

Choose one small boundary you can practice today. It might involve saying no, asking for time to yourself or speaking up gently when something feels uncomfortable.

Grounding line

My boundaries honor my worth.

DAY FOUR. NAMING UNMET NEEDS

Reflection

Many people grow up believing that expressing their needs makes them difficult or demanding. In truth, needs are natural and essential. When you do not acknowledge them, they find ways to surface through stress, longing or emotional overwhelm. Today you will give your needs a voice.

Prompt

Write about a need that has been consistently unmet in your life. Describe how it feels not to have that need fulfilled and what it would mean to have it honored.

Exercise

Say aloud one sentence that acknowledges your need. It can be gentle and simple. Allow yourself to feel the truth of it without judgment.

Grounding line

My needs are valid and worthy of care.

DAY FIVE. RECOGNIZING SELF TALK

Reflection

Your inner voice has the power to lift you or tear you down. It can reflect love or echo old pain. Becoming aware of your self talk helps you understand how your past influences the way you treat yourself. Today you will listen closely to the words you direct inward.

Prompt

Write down the thoughts you often say to yourself during difficult moments. Notice the tone. Ask yourself where those words came from and whether they reflect your truth.

Exercise

Choose one harsh thought and rewrite it in a kinder voice. Say it to yourself whenever old patterns surface.

Grounding line

I speak to myself with gentleness.

DAY SIX. EXPLORING WHAT YOU BELIEVED YOU DESERVED

Reflection

Our sense of deserving is often shaped long before we understand its influence. If you believed you deserved very little, you may have accepted unkind behavior or overextended yourself to earn love. If you believed you had to prove your worth, you may have stayed in situations that drained you. Today is about seeing these beliefs clearly.

Prompt

Write about what you once believed you deserved in relationships. Explore where these beliefs came from and how they influenced your choices.

Exercise

Create a new belief about what you deserve in love. Keep it simple and true. Repeat it slowly until it feels familiar.

Grounding line

I deserve love that feels safe and steady.

DAY SEVEN. GETTING CLEAR ABOUT WHAT IS NOT SERVING YOU

Reflection

Old habits, fears and beliefs can follow you for years without being questioned. They may have served a purpose at one time, but as you grow, they can become barriers to the life and love you want. Today marks a turning point. You will identify what is ready to be released so you can create space for something healthier.

Prompt

Write about something in your life that no longer serves your emotional wellbeing. Describe how it affects you and why you are ready to let it go.

Exercise

Imagine placing this thing in your hands. Close your eyes and picture yourself gently setting it down. Breathe deeply as you release it, even if only symbolically.

Grounding line

I am ready to let go of what weighs me down.

Notes

WEEK TWO. Healing and Release

Healing rarely arrives in a single moment. It is a series of small shifts, slow realizations and quiet releases that happen inside you over time. This week invites you to soften the places where you have been holding emotional tension. You spent the first week becoming aware of your patterns and truths. Now you begin the work of loosening their grip.

Healing is not forgetting. Healing is remembering without losing yourself in the memory. It is feeling the ache without letting it define you. It is looking at your past with honesty and compassion instead of shame or regret. Many people believe they need closure from others in order to heal. Real closure often comes from within. It comes from choosing to let go of stories that have hurt you and from accepting that the past cannot be changed. Only your relationship to it can.

Releasing old emotions can feel uncomfortable because they have become familiar. Even painful patterns can feel strangely safe when you have known them for a long time. This week helps you step into unfamiliar territory. Here, you will practice letting go of comparisons that undermine your confidence. You will create space for grief instead of resisting it. You will forgive yourself for choices you made when you did not know better. You will rewrite beliefs that have limited your growth. You will understand how attachment has shaped your relationships. You will untangle the habit of people pleasing. You will breathe deeper as you reclaim your space and your voice.

Healing is not linear. Some days will feel light and freeing. Other days you might feel tender or uncertain. This is normal. Every emotional shift stirs something inside you. Instead of resisting the discomfort, approach it with gentle curiosity. Your heart is learning a new way of being.

Think of this week as the slow release of pressure. The softening of clenched places. The moment when your heart stops bracing for impact and begins trusting the possibility of peace. Let these pages hold you through the process.

DAY EIGHT. LETTING GO OF COMPARISONS

Reflection

Comparison is a quiet thief. It steals your confidence, your joy and your sense of worth. It can happen without you noticing. You might compare your healing timeline to someone else's or your past relationships to what you see in others. You might look at people who seem happy and wonder why your heart feels heavier. Comparison makes you forget your own path. Today is about returning to yourself.

Prompt

Write about a recent moment when you compared yourself to someone else. Describe what you felt and what story your mind created in that moment.

Exercise

Place your hand on your heart and speak one truth about your own journey. Let it be simple. Let it be yours. Repeat it slowly until it feels like it belongs to you again.

Grounding line

My path is mine alone and it is enough.

DAY NINE. MAKING SPACE FOR GRIEF

Reflection

Grief is not only for loss of life. It is for the loss of dreams, hopes, versions of yourself and relationships that changed or ended. Many people try to rush grief away because it feels heavy. Yet grief is simply love looking for somewhere to go. When you allow grief to exist without fighting it, it moves through you instead of staying trapped within you. Today is about letting your heart feel without fear.

Prompt

Write about something you have been grieving, whether quietly or openly. Let your emotions speak without trying to tidy them.

Exercise

Sit in stillness for a few breaths. Place both hands over your heart and acknowledge your grief with compassion. Tell yourself it is safe to feel what you feel.

Grounding line

My grief is a natural expression of love.

DAY TEN. FORGIVING YOURSELF

Reflection

Self forgiveness is one of the most powerful forms of healing. Many people carry shame for choices they made out of fear, loneliness or confusion. You did the best you knew how to do with the awareness you had at the time. Holding yourself hostage to old mistakes keeps you tied to the past. Forgiveness does not erase what happened. It releases the self blame that prevents you from moving forward.

Prompt

Write about something you have struggled to forgive yourself for. Let your words come from honesty rather than judgment.

Exercise

Write one sentence that expresses understanding toward your past self. Speak to yourself the way you would speak to someone you love who was hurting.

Grounding line

I offer myself compassion and release.

DAY ELEVEN. REWRITING LIMITING BELiefs

Reflection

Limiting beliefs form quietly and often early. They might tell you that you are hard to love, that your needs are too much or that you always end up hurt. These beliefs become self fulfilling because they shape how you behave and what you accept. Rewriting them is an act of liberation. Today you will challenge the beliefs that have kept you small and replace them with ones that support your growth.

Prompt

Write down a belief about yourself that has held you back in relationships or in life. Describe where it came from and how it has influenced your choices.

Exercise

Rewrite the belief in a way that supports your healing. Keep it short, true and compassionate. Repeat it aloud until it feels possible.

Grounding line

I am allowed to grow beyond my old beliefs.

DAY TWELVE. UNDERSTANDING ATTACHMENT

Reflection

Attachment styles influence the way you love, the way you react and the way you cope with uncertainty. Whether anxious, avoidant, secure or a blend, your attachment style is a response to your history, not a permanent truth about who you are. Understanding it helps you make sense of your emotional reactions and choose healthier ways of relating. Today you will observe your own attachment tendencies with curiosity.

Prompt

Reflect on how you tend to respond when connection feels threatened. Do you pull closer, pull away or freeze. Describe a moment that revealed this pattern.

Exercise

Write a gentle reminder to yourself about what you need during moments of emotional tension. Offer guidance rather than criticism.

Grounding line

I am learning to relate with clarity and calm.

DAY THIRTEEN. RELEASING THE HABIT OF PEOPLE PLEASING

Reflection

People pleasing often forms as a survival strategy. You may have learned that keeping the peace kept you safe or that being agreeable earned affection. Over time, this pattern can make you disappear inside your own life. You deserve to be seen. You deserve relationships where your needs matter. Today is about loosening the instinct to please others at the cost of yourself.

Prompt

Write about a time you silenced your needs to avoid conflict or keep someone comfortable. Describe what you felt and what it cost you.

Exercise

Practice choosing yourself in one small way today. It might be a moment of rest, a gentle no or a clear expression of preference.

Grounding line

I honor myself by honoring my needs.

DAY FOURTEEN. CREATING EMOTIONAL SPACE

Reflection

Healing requires room to breathe. If your heart has been crowded by past hurts, constant overthinking or emotional clutter, it may feel heavy and overwhelmed. Emotional space allows you to reset. It gives you room to see your life clearly and choose what nourishes you. Today you create space within yourself by releasing what is ready to loosen.

Prompt

Write about the emotional clutter you have been holding. This may include expectations, memories, fears or responsibilities that are not yours to carry.

Exercise

Take five slow breaths. With each exhale, imagine your heart softening. Visualize yourself creating space for peace, clarity and new beginnings.

Grounding line

My heart has room to heal and open.

Notes

WEEK THREE.
Rebuilding Self Worth

By the time you reach this third week, you have already done the deep work of looking inward. You have explored your patterns, your needs, your grief and your beliefs. You have softened the weight of old emotions and made space for healing. Now you enter a chapter focused on rebuilding. This week is about choosing yourself in ways you might have forgotten to choose yourself before. It is about recognizing your strengths, trusting your inner wisdom and slowly stepping back into your own light.

Self worth is not a single moment of clarity. It is a practice. It grows through the choices you make each day. It strengthens as you begin to treat yourself with respect and kindness. It becomes more rooted each time you honor your needs, protect your boundaries and speak to yourself with compassion. Many people think self worth comes from success or admiration or love from others. True self worth comes from the way you show up for yourself, especially when life feels uncertain.

During this week, you will reflect on the small victories that often go unnoticed. You will learn to see your inner strength even while healing. You will begin to rebuild trust with yourself by keeping simple promises. You will take steps toward living more intentionally rather than reactively. You will identify the habits and choices that support the person you are becoming. You will also give yourself permission to rest, because worthiness is not something you earn through effort. It is something you remember.

You may notice moments of resistance during this week. A part of you might still believe you are not worthy enough, not ready enough or not strong enough. Let these thoughts surface, but do not let them drive you. You are not trying to become someone new. You are reconnecting with the version of yourself that has always existed beneath the noise of fear and doubt.

Self worth is built through repetition. Every time you choose honesty over fear, compassion over self criticism, boundaries over self abandonment or rest over burnout, you strengthen your foundation. You become someone who shows up for yourself consistently. This is what creates confidence that lasts. Not ego, not perfection, but steady self connection.

These next seven days will support you in rebuilding the parts of you that forgot how capable you truly are. They will encourage you to acknowledge your growth, celebrate your resilience and trust the unfolding of your own process. Allow yourself to lean into this gentler, more loving way of relating to yourself. It will change the way you move through the world.

DAY FIFTEEN. RECOGNIZING YOUR STRENGTHS

Reflection

Sometimes the hardest thing to see is your own strength. Pain can blur your view. Healing can make you feel fragile even when you are becoming stronger each day. Today is about shifting your focus from what has been difficult to what has been resilient within you. Strength is not loud. Strength is the quiet persistence that keeps you moving forward even when the path is unclear. It is the willingness to reflect, to learn, to heal and to hope again.

Prompt

Write about a moment in your life when you showed strength, whether or not anyone noticed. Describe what you did, how you felt and what that moment reveals about you now.

Exercise

Place your hand on your heart and speak one sentence acknowledging the resilience inside you. Say it slowly until it feels true.

Grounding line

There is strength in me that I have not yet fully recognized.

DAY SIXTEEN. CELEBRATING SMALL WINS

Reflection

Growth often happens in small steps, not giant leaps. You may overlook these steps because they seem too minor or too quiet to matter. But small wins create momentum. They reinforce the belief that you are capable of change. When you celebrate them, you strengthen your self worth by reminding yourself that your efforts count. Today you will honor the little things you have done to support your healing.

Prompt

Reflect on the small wins you have had during this journal journey so far. They might be emotional shifts, clearer boundaries or moments of courage. Write them down with appreciation.

Exercise

Choose one small win from your list and take a moment to sit with the pride it brings. Let yourself feel the truth that progress is happening.

Grounding line

Every small step I take holds power and meaning.

DAY SEVENTEEN. REBUILDING TRUST WITH YOURSELF

Reflection

Trust is the foundation of self worth. When you trust yourself, you feel grounded and confident in your choices. When trust is shaky, you may feel uncertain, anxious or dependent on outside reassurance. Many people struggle with self trust because they have been taught to ignore their intuition or silence their needs. Rebuilding trust with yourself begins with keeping simple promises. It is a gradual process that strengthens each time you follow through with gentle consistency.

Prompt

Write about a time when you ignored your intuition and later wished you had listened. Describe what held you back and what that experience taught you.

Exercise

Make one small promise to yourself today. Keep it simple and achievable. It might be pausing before reacting or taking a moment to breathe before making a decision. Follow through with it fully.

Grounding line

I strengthen my self trust through consistent and gentle commitment.

DAY EIGHTEEN. HONORING YOUR NEED FOR REST

Reflection

Many people tie their worth to productivity or doing. When this happens, rest begins to feel like laziness or failure rather than nourishment. True self worth includes the belief that your value does not depend on how much you accomplish. Your heart needs rest in the same way your body does. Rest allows your emotions to settle and your mind to clear. Today is about recognizing rest as an essential piece of your healing.

Prompt

Write about your relationship with rest. Do you allow yourself to rest without guilt. Do you push yourself past your limits. Explore the beliefs that shape how you treat your own energy.

Exercise

Give yourself permission to rest today, even for a few minutes. Close your eyes, breathe slowly and allow your body to soften without asking anything of you.

Grounding line

Resting is an act of honoring my worth, not avoiding my life.

DAY NINETEEN. CHOOSING SUPPORTIVE HABITS

Reflection

Habits shape your emotional landscape. Some habits nourish your wellbeing while others drain your energy or reinforce old patterns. Choosing supportive habits does not require dramatic changes. It begins with small actions that remind your heart it deserves care. Today you will reflect on the habits that help you feel grounded and the ones that pull you away from yourself.

Prompt

Write about one habit that supports your wellbeing and one habit that drains you. Describe how each affects your sense of self worth.

Exercise

Choose one supportive habit to practice today. Make it gentle and realistic. It might be drinking water mindfully, journaling for a moment or stepping outside for fresh air.

Grounding line

I choose habits that support the person I am becoming.

DAY TWENTY. LISTENING TO YOUR INNER VOICE

Reflection

Inside you there is a voice that knows what you need, what you desire and what feels right. This inner voice may have been silenced by fear, doubt or the need to please others. Rebuilding self worth requires learning to hear this voice again. It speaks quietly but clearly. Today you will give it space to rise without being overshadowed by old insecurities.

Prompt

Write a letter from your inner voice to your current self. Allow it to share guidance, encouragement or clarity without judgment.

Exercise

Sit in silence for a few breaths and notice what thoughts emerge that feel calm and grounded. These thoughts often reflect your true inner guidance.

Grounding line

My inner voice speaks with clarity and wisdom.

DAY TWENTY ONE. CLAIMING YOUR VALUE

Reflection

Self worth becomes stronger when you consciously claim your value. This does not mean forcing confidence or pretending you never struggle. It means acknowledging that you deserve love, respect and emotional safety. It means believing that your needs matter as much as anyone else's. Claiming your value is an ongoing practice that shapes the way you show up in relationships and in life. Today you will take a step toward owning your worth.

Prompt

Write about the qualities that make you valuable. Focus on your character, your kindness, your growth and the ways you show up for others and yourself.

Exercise

Speak one sentence aloud that affirms your value. Even if it feels unfamiliar, allow yourself to say it slowly. Let the truth of it settle into your body.

Grounding line

I am worthy of love, respect and a life that feels good to my heart.

Notes

WEEK FOUR. Choosing Healthier Love

You have spent three weeks turning inward, clearing emotional space and rebuilding your connection to yourself. Now you step into the final week of this journey, where everything you have learned begins to settle into your heart. This chapter is about choosing love from a grounded place. Not from fear, not from old wounds, not from the pressure to fill a void. Healthy love is created when you know your worth and honor it.

Many people enter relationships before they understand their needs or boundaries. Others choose partners who reflect their wounds rather than their growth. Some settle for patterns they would never encourage a friend to accept. This week asks you to pause and consider what love should feel like. Not what you were taught. Not what you tolerated in the past. What love feels like when it is safe, steady, respectful and nourishing.

Healthy love begins with clarity. You will explore your non negotiables, the values that matter most to you and the emotional qualities that create true connection. You will reflect on red flags and green flags without judgment. You will consider how you want to show up in future relationships and what reciprocity means to you. You will also explore the fears that arise when something feels good, because many people unconsciously sabotage healthy love when it appears. The familiar can feel safer than the good. This chapter helps you shift that pattern.

Choosing healthier love does not require a partner. It requires intention. As you move through these reflections, you are strengthening your inner compass. You are learning to choose connection that brings peace rather than chaos. You are learning to trust what feels aligned. You are choosing truth over attachment, growth over comfort and respect over longing.

This week is not about rushing into new love. It is about preparing your heart to recognize the kind of love that matches your healing. You will look at love through a lens of wholeness rather than fear. When your self worth is rooted and your emotional clarity is strong, love becomes something you choose consciously rather than stumble into.

Allow this final week to guide your heart gently toward the relationships that honor who you are becoming. You have done the work. Now you begin to harvest the benefits.

DAY TWENTY TWO. DEFINING HEALTHY LOVE

Reflection

Healthy love feels like ease in your body. It feels like being accepted without having to shrink or stretch to fit someone else's expectations. It is not perfect or smooth all the time, but it is honest, respectful and consistent. Today you will explore what healthy love means to you. This definition will guide your choices moving forward.

Prompt

Write about the qualities that make love feel healthy, safe and nourishing for you. Describe what your heart needs in order to thrive in connection.

Exercise

Place your hand over your heart and say one sentence about the kind of love you want to create. Let it be simple and sincere.

Grounding line

I welcome love that brings ease, truth and steady connection.

DAY TWENTY THREE. RECOGNIZING RED AND GREEN FLAGS

Reflection

Red flags often feel familiar because they echo past wounds. Green flags can feel unfamiliar when you are used to inconsistency or emotional distance. Today is about noticing both without judgment. Red flags show you where your boundaries need to strengthen. Green flags show you what your heart is learning to trust.

Prompt

Write about a red flag you have ignored in the past and what it taught you. Then write about a green flag you appreciate and want more of in your relationships.

Exercise

Take a quiet moment and imagine a future connection where green flags are the norm. Notice how your body responds to that vision.

Grounding line

I see clearly what aligns with my growth and what does not.

DAY TWENTY FOUR. DISCOVERING EMOTIONAL COMPATIBILITY

Reflection

Attraction is not enough to sustain a relationship. Emotional compatibility influences whether two people can move through life as a team. It includes communication style, emotional availability, conflict resolution and shared values. Today you will explore what compatibility means for you so you can choose partners who align with your emotional rhythm.

Prompt

Reflect on what emotional compatibility feels like. Describe the qualities and behaviors that help you feel understood, valued and emotionally safe.

Exercise

Close your eyes and imagine a relationship where compatibility is present. Notice the calmness of that connection and how it affects your sense of self.

Grounding line

I am aligned with relationships that support my emotional wellbeing.

DAY TWENTY FIVE. HONORING YOUR NON NEGOTIABLES

Reflection

Non negotiables are the boundaries that protect your self worth. They are not demands. They are standards that honor your emotional health. Many people ignore their non negotiables out of loneliness or hope that things will change. When you honor them, you create a foundation for sustainable love.

Prompt

Write down the qualities, behaviors and values that you cannot compromise on in relationships. Let this be an honest reflection of what protects your peace.

Exercise

Read your non negotiables slowly. Ask yourself if you have honored them in the past and how you want to honor them moving forward.

Grounding line

My non negotiables protect my heart and my peace.

DAY TWENTY SIX. PRACTICING RECEIVING HEALTHY AFFECTION

Reflection

For those who have been hurt, receiving healthy love can feel uncomfortable. When someone is kind or consistent, you might question their intentions or pull away. This is often a sign of old wounds, not lack of desire. Today you will explore what it means to receive love without fear. Allowing people to care for you is part of healing.

Prompt

Write about a time when someone offered genuine care or affection and you felt unsure how to receive it. Explore what came up for you emotionally.

Exercise

Write a sentence affirming your ability to receive healthy love without fear. Let the words sink in as you breathe slowly.

Grounding line

I allow love to reach me with openness and trust.

DAY TWENTY SEVEN. UNDERSTANDING HOW YOU SHOW UP IN LOVE

Reflection

Every person has a unique way of showing up in relationships. Some lead with caretaking. Some lead with independence. Others seek closeness while fearing vulnerability. Today you will reflect on the energy you bring to love. Understanding your patterns helps you create connections that feel balanced and reciprocal.

Prompt

Write about how you tend to show up in relationships. Consider your communication style, your expectations, your fears and your strengths. Let this be an honest exploration rather than a critique.

Exercise

Choose one intention for how you want to show up in future relationships. Keep it simple and grounded in self respect.

Grounding line

I show up in love with clarity, balance and honesty.

DAY TWENTY EIGHT. PREPARING YOUR HEART FOR A NEW CHAPTER

Reflection

Your heart has grown, softened and strengthened through these weeks. Whether or not you are ready for new love, you are ready for a new chapter. This chapter may involve deeper self connection, healthier boundaries or relationships that reflect your worth. Today is about acknowledging your readiness for what comes next, even if the details are unknown.

Prompt

Write about what you feel ready for now. It may be peace, clarity, healthier relationships or a renewed connection with yourself. Let your heart speak freely.

Exercise

Imagine taking one small step into this new chapter. Picture yourself moving forward with confidence and calm. Breathe deeply into that image.

Grounding line

My heart is ready for the next version of my life.

Notes

Part 3
Completion and Integration

Healing is a slow unfolding. It rarely arrives in one defining moment. Instead, it reveals itself through the way you think, speak, choose and respond. This final section of your journey invites you to look back with honesty and compassion, to recognize how far you have come and to anchor the emotional shifts that have taken shape within you.

During these thirty days, you have explored the layers of your inner world. You have learned to witness your thoughts without judgment. You have acknowledged your grief, softened your defenses and released the stories that no longer reflected your truth. You have rebuilt parts of yourself that were ignored or forgotten. And above all, you have learned to listen to your own heart with gentleness.

Completion does not mean perfection. Integration does not mean final answers. You are not closing the door on your healing. You are stepping into the next chapter of your life with greater clarity, deeper awareness and rooted self worth.

This part of the journal asks you to gather everything you have learned so that you can carry it forward. You will reflect on the shifts that have taken place within you. You will identify the needs that guide your sense of wellbeing. You will acknowledge the patterns you have released and the ones you now refuse to revisit. You will define what healthy love means to you in the present moment, not based on old wounds but on your growing self respect.

This chapter is your landing place. It is your breath after the climb. It is your chance to honor the work you have done and to envision how you want to continue showing up for yourself long after these pages are complete.

Let this be a soft closing. A gentle transition. A space where everything comes together.

Your Thirty Day Reflection

There is a point in every healing journey where you look back and realize you are no longer the person you were when you began. You see how your mind has shifted, how your body holds less tension, how your voice feels steadier when you speak your truth. You notice that your longing for clarity has started to transform into clarity itself. You feel more connected to your needs and less afraid of honoring them.

Reflection helps you see your growth clearly. It makes your healing visible. It allows you to witness the parts of yourself that have resurfaced from beneath the noise of old patterns. This is where your thirty days settle into place.

Settle into your body for a moment. Allow your breath to lengthen. Allow your heart to soften. You have arrived at the threshold of completion.

Below you will find a series of guided reflections, each designed to illuminate the ways you have grown during this process.

Let your answers flow freely and tenderly. This is not about being poetic or precise. It is about being honest.

What shifted inside you during this process

Reflection

Change can be quiet. Sometimes it arrives little by little, like a soft rearranging of the pieces inside you. Other times it arrives all at once through sudden clarity. Whatever shape your transformation has taken, something has shifted. Something has loosened or opened or strengthened. Today you will look directly at that shift.

Prompts

What do you feel now that you did not feel before.

What have you let go of, even slightly.

What truth became clearer to you over these thirty days.

Exercise

Sit for one minute with your eyes closed. Place your hand over your chest and notice the steadiness beneath your palm. Imagine this steadiness as the foundation you have built. Let your body recognize that you have changed, even if the change is subtle.

Grounding line

I honor the shifts that have taken place within me.

What you now know about your needs

Reflection

Needs are the compass of your emotional world. They point you toward what nourishes you and away from what harms you. During the past four weeks, you have learned to notice your needs rather than bury them. You have learned that your needs matter just as much as the needs of others. This part of your reflection helps you define those needs clearly.

Prompts

What needs surfaced most often as you wrote in this journal.

What do you require in order to feel emotionally safe.

What do you need from yourself in order to stay grounded.

What do you need from others that you are no longer afraid to name.

Exercise

Write a short letter to yourself listing the needs you promise to honor moving forward. Let this letter be both gentle and firm. Keep it somewhere you can return to when you feel disconnected from your truth.

Grounding line

My needs are worthy of attention, respect and compassion.

What patterns you have released

Reflection

Patterns often form as a response to pain. They can feel protective at first, but over time they begin to limit your emotional freedom. Throughout this journey, you have recognized the patterns that kept you small or stuck. You have begun loosening them, even if they are not entirely gone. Releasing does not mean everything has healed completely. It means you no longer wish to be guided by old pain.

Prompts

What emotional pattern do you feel less attached to now.

What belief have you outgrown.

What habit or reflexive reaction has softened through this process.

What old story no longer feels like it belongs to you.

Exercise

On a separate sheet of paper, write down one pattern you are committed to releasing. Fold the paper and place it in an envelope. Seal it. This symbolic act represents your willingness to step out of the past. You can keep the envelope or let it go. Your intention is what matters.

Grounding line

I release what once protected me but no longer serves my wellbeing.

What healthy love looks like for you now

Reflection

Your understanding of love has likely shifted as you moved through awareness, healing and rebuilding. You are seeing love through a clearer lens now, one shaped by self worth instead of longing. Healthy love is not a fantasy or a perfect storyline. It is a daily choice rooted in honesty, reciprocity and emotional safety. It grows from within you first, and then extends outward.

Prompts

What qualities do you now believe are essential in healthy love.

How do you want to feel in a relationship.

What behaviors do you no longer accept.

What does partnership look like when it supports your growth instead of your fears.

Exercise

Visualize the version of yourself who is ready to receive and give healthy love. Picture how you walk, how you speak, how you hold your boundaries, how your heart feels. Let this vision be a reminder of the love you are capable of cultivating.

Grounding line

Healthy love begins with the way I love myself.

INTEGRATION: MAKING YOUR GROWTH LAST

You have reached the final stage of this journey, but emotional integration continues for as long as you choose it. Integration is the practice of weaving your new insights into your daily life. It is the process of turning knowledge into action, clarity into boundaries, awareness into self protection, and healing into long term growth.

Integrating your healing means you choose yourself consistently.

It means you listen to the quiet signals of your body instead of overriding them.

It means you speak up even when your voice shakes.

It means you allow rest without guilt.

It means you recognize the difference between longing and compatibility.

It means you honor your needs with the same respect you offer others.

Below is your final integrative reflection, designed to bring all your emotional work together. Let these pages hold your truth.

Integration Reflection: How you will move forward

Reflection

Your healing does not end with these pages. It deepens through the choices you make after you close this book. Integration asks you to consider how you will continue honoring your needs, your boundaries and your self worth in the real world.

Prompts

How will you continue supporting your emotional wellbeing.

What practices helped you most and how will you carry them with you.

How will you respond to old triggers if they reappear.

What commitments are you making to your future self.

Exercise

Write a brief manifesto for the next chapter of your life.

This can be a paragraph or a single sentence. Let it express your values, your intentions and your sense of self worth. Place it somewhere you will see often.

Grounding line

I continue forward with clarity, self trust and an open heart.

Notes

Your New Self Worth Blueprint

This section gathers everything you have learned and turns it into a living map you can return to whenever you feel uncertain or disconnected. A blueprint is not a rigid plan. It is a grounding place, a reminder of who you are when you are rooted in your truth. Think of this as the clearest reflection of your emotional foundation after thirty days of healing, clarity and awareness.

Take your time. Let these pages unfold slowly. Speak honestly and gently to yourself. You are not trying to craft a perfect identity. You are bringing forward the truest version of you, the one who knows what she deserves, what she values and how she wishes to move through love and life.

Settle into your breath. Let your body soften. Let your heart speak freely.

Your Strengths

Every person carries strengths that remain invisible until they are acknowledged. Some strengths emerge through hardship. Others develop through tenderness, resilience or the simple act of continuing on days that felt heavy. Now is the moment to name the qualities that make you capable, compassionate and deeply yourself.

Reflect on what has carried you through this journey. Consider the ways you have shown courage, patience, softness, honesty or determination. Write about the qualities within you that make you someone who loves deeply, learns willingly and heals bravely.

Allow your strengths to rise without shrinking them. Let them sit proudly on the page. These qualities are part of your foundation.

Your Boundaries

Boundaries are the borders of your emotional wellbeing. They protect your heart from shrinking into old patterns. They keep you aligned with your values and your needs. Your boundaries are not defenses. They are declarations of self respect.

Begin by writing about the limits you now understand more clearly. These may include the amount of emotional labor you are willing to carry, the way you expect to be spoken to or the energy you will no longer extend without reciprocity. Reflect on the boundaries that help you feel safe, steady and respected.

Write them as truths, not wishes. Let them reflect your growth rather than your fears. These boundaries guide how you relate to others and how you relate to yourself.

Your Values

Values guide every choice you make. They determine how you move through relationships, how you communicate and what you prioritize. When you are anchored in your values, your decisions feel clear rather than chaotic. Values offer a sense of direction even when emotions feel uncertain.

Reflect on the values that have become clearer to you during this journey. Perhaps you value honesty, kindness, consistency or personal growth. Maybe you value emotional safety, mutual respect or balanced connection. Write about the principles that matter most to you and why they feel essential to your wellbeing.

Your values form the core of your emotional identity. Knowing them keeps you aligned with the life you want to create.

Your Relationship Vision

Now that you understand yourself with greater clarity, imagine the kind of love that aligns with your growth. This is not about designing a perfect partner. It is about understanding the shape of a relationship that supports your heart rather than burdens it.

Write about what partnership looks like for you now. Picture the emotional tone of the connection. Consider the way communication feels, the way conflict is handled and the way affection is expressed. Imagine a relationship where you feel seen rather than overlooked, valued rather than tolerated, safe rather than anxious.

Describe how you show up in this connection and how your partner shows up for you. Let this vision be grounded, warm and honest. You are shaping a love that mirrors your healing, not your wounds.

Your Emotional Standards

Emotional standards are the expectations you hold for how you want to feel within yourself and within your relationships. Standards are not demands. They are reflections of your self worth.

Write about how you want to feel in connection. Perhaps you want to feel calm, respected, supported or cherished. Maybe you want to feel free to express your needs without fear. Consider what you no longer accept in your emotional world and what you expect instead.

Your emotional standards guide every decision you make. They help you recognize when something is aligned and when something is taking you away from your truth.

Your Daily Practices for Clarity

Clarity is not a one time achievement. It is a daily practice. The habits you create will keep you connected to yourself long after this journal is complete.

Reflect on the practices that helped you feel grounded during these thirty days. You may have found comfort in journaling, in mindful breathing, in quiet reflection, in gentle movement or in speaking kindly to yourself. You may have noticed how much lighter you feel when you honor your needs without guilt.

Write about the practices you want to carry forward. Describe how you will integrate them into your days with ease rather than pressure. These practices are the threads that keep you connected to your self worth.

Bringing It All Together

Your blueprint is a living guide. It is not meant to restrict you. It is meant to support you as you continue to grow. Return to it whenever you need reassurance, clarity or grounding. Let it remind you of who you became during these thirty days and who you are still becoming.

Take a moment to read through everything you have written. Notice how whole it feels. Notice how honest it sounds. This blueprint is your gift to yourself, born from your courage to look inward and your willingness to heal.

When you are ready, place your hand over your heart and breathe deeply. Recognize the strength it took to arrive here. Recognize the truth of your worth. Recognize the path you are stepping into with clarity and confidence.

> The blueprint is yours.
> Your healing is yours.
> Your future is yours.

Notes

Your Next Steps

Healing continues long after the last page of this journal. It grows through repetition, gentle awareness and the choices you make each day. You have spent thirty days learning to listen to yourself with patience and compassion. You have softened old patterns, released heavy emotions and rebuilt parts of your self worth that had been waiting for attention. Now you step into a future shaped by these shifts.

This final chapter offers a tender guide for moving forward. Nothing here is meant to feel demanding. These are soft invitations, steady reminders and ways to stay connected to the work you have already done. Think of this as a continuation rather than an ending.

Take a breath. Let your shoulders drop. Let this next step feel natural.

Monthly Reflection Ideas

Reflection does not need to be daily to be meaningful. One gentle check in each month can help you stay aligned with your growth without overwhelming your routine. These reflections allow you to notice how your needs change, how your boundaries hold and how your heart responds to new experiences.

Set aside a quiet moment once a month. Bring a cup of tea or sit somewhere peaceful. Ask yourself what has felt nourishing this month and what has felt draining. Consider where you honored your boundaries and where you abandoned yourself. Look at the relationships around you. Notice who adds ease to your life and who brings tension or confusion.

You might also reflect on any emotional triggers that resurfaced. Noticing them does not mean you are failing. It means you are paying attention. Growth involves revisiting old feelings with new awareness. Each time you pause to reflect, you strengthen your connection to yourself.

Let monthly reflection be an act of care rather than analysis. This is a moment for honesty, calm and curiosity.

Practicing an Emotional Reset Long Term

An emotional reset is not a one time event. It is a lifelong practice of pausing, breathing and choosing again. Some days you will feel grounded and clear. Other days you may slip into old patterns. Both experiences are part of healing.

To practice emotional reset long term, return to the habits that supported you during these thirty days. Keep noticing your emotions without judgment. When something feels heavy, ask yourself what you need rather than pushing the feeling aside. When you feel triggered, offer yourself patience instead of criticism. When you feel unsure, pause long enough to listen to your inner voice.

You can also create small reset rituals for yourself. This might be a few minutes of journaling to release thoughts that feel cluttered. It might be a slow walk to reconnect with your body. It might be choosing rest when your heart feels overstretched. Resetting is not about starting over. It is about realigning with who you are in this moment.

Allow yourself to course correct without shame. Healing expands through gentleness.

Revisiting This Journal

These pages are always available when you need them. Healing is not linear, and there may be times in the future when you feel lost, overwhelmed or disconnected from yourself. Returning to this journal is not a step backward. It is a return to your foundation.

You can revisit an entire week or simply a single prompt that once brought clarity. You can write in the margins, add new reflections or even restart the journey from the beginning. Each time you come back, you will meet yourself at a deeper level. You will notice changes you did not see the first time. You will find new meaning in old passages because you are healing in layers.

Let this journal be a companion, not a task. Let it be a safe place where your heart can land whenever it needs a quieter way to speak.

A Closing Note

You have given yourself thirty days of presence, honesty and tenderness. You have chosen to understand yourself rather than judge yourself. You have listened to what your heart has been trying to say. These acts are powerful. They shape the life you create from this moment forward.

There will be days when you feel light and open, and days when old fears return. This is normal. Healing is a spiral, returning you to familiar places with deeper wisdom each time. Trust yourself. Trust your growth. Trust the version of you who showed up on every page of this journal with sincerity.

Carry your clarity gently. Carry your boundaries with pride. Carry your worth as something steady and unshakeable.

This is not the end of your healing. It is the beginning of a life lived with intention, self respect and love that reflects who you truly are.

Notes

About the Author

Eden Clarke writes from a place of lived experience, emotional honesty and a deep belief in the possibility of healing. Her work centers on self compassion, inner clarity and the quiet strength that grows when we learn to listen to our own hearts. Eden's gentle approach reflects years of observing how people heal, how they love and how they reclaim the pieces of themselves they once lost in the noise of life.

She is passionate about creating spaces where individuals feel safe to explore their inner world. Her writing is shaped by a desire to help others understand their emotions, release old patterns and step into relationships that honor their worth. Eden believes that healing is not about perfection but about sincerity, courage and steady self connection.

When she is not writing, she spends time in nature, reading thoughtfully chosen books and connecting with people who value depth and authenticity. She finds inspiration in quiet

About the Author

moments, in heartfelt conversations and in the simple truth that every heart is capable of beginning again.

Eden's work invites readers to slow down, breathe and trust the wisdom within themselves. Her hope is that this journal becomes a companion for anyone ready to rebuild, rediscover and return to their own light.

Notes Pages

These pages are here for your thoughts, reflections, insights and anything your heart wants to unravel or remember. There is no structure to follow and no expectation for what should appear here. This space belongs entirely to you.

Use it to capture ideas that rise as you complete the journal, moments of clarity that appear unexpectedly or reminders you want to carry forward. You may choose to write freely, create lists of things you want to release or record memories that deserve gentleness.

Let these pages hold whatever you need them to hold. They are a quiet place for your voice, your truth and your continued journey.

Notes

Notes

Notes

Notes

Notes

Notes

Notes

Notes

Notes

Notes

www.ingramcontent.com/pod-product-compliance
Lightning Source LLC
Chambersburg PA
CBHW052107070526
44584CB00017B/2380